The Man Who Created Narnia

Ten Things About

C.S. Lewis

&

What Makes Him Unique

The Man Who Created Narnia

Ten Things About

C.S. Lewis

&

What Makes Him Unique

Reggie Weems

Unless otherwise noted, Scripture quotations are taken from The Holy Bible, English Standard Version® (ESV®) Copyright © 2001 by Crossway, a publishing ministry of Good News Publishers. All rights reserved. ESV Text Edition: 2016

Copyright © 2019, Reggie Weems

www.10thingsabout.org

All rights reserved. No part of this book may be reproduced, scanned, or distributed in any printed or electronic form without permission.

First Edition: 2019

ISBN 978-1-7343452-2-3

To buy quantities of this book at a special rate for bulk use, email info@greatwriting.org

Great Writing Publications
www.greatwriting.org
Taylors, SC

Table of Contents

	About the Series	7
	Introduction	9
1	Ireland	11
2	Childhood	16
3	Death	21
4	Schools	27
5	Joy	34
6	Atheism	39
7	Conversion	44
8	People	49
9	Romantic Apologetics	56
10	Eschatology	62
	Conclusion	69
	About the Author	71
	Acknowledgments	72
Endnotes		73

To my mother

Virginia Weems,

the best mother in the world and the person who taught me to love books

TEN THINGS is a series of books offering biblical encouragement and practical direction on matters of concern to modern Christians who are seeking Bible-saturated, Christ-centered, Spirit-empowered, practical guidance. The series is published in an electronic and print format for quick, private, and easy access.

The books are brief and to the point, enabling readers to access immediate help and genuine hope for real-life situations. They are also written in a pastoral tone intended to shepherd hearts and minds toward Christ-centered, whole-life transformation.

This encouragement is not intended to and cannot replace personal pastoral counsel or the accountability of living transparently in Christian fellowship with other believers. Both are invaluable to you. A particular book may inspire a reader, but lifelong change only occurs in the context of Spirit-empowered living in biblical community.

Because of its biblical and simple approach, pastors may also employ the series to disciple church leaders who minister to God's flock.

Introduction

Every book makes a promise and my promise is to introduce you to C.S. Lewis, who in 1947, was referred to as "a best-selling author and one of the most influential spokesmen for Christianity in the English-speaking world."[1] Seventy-two years later, Jack[2] is still one of the best-selling Christian authors in the world and his 21st century influence is unavoidable in the Western hemisphere.[3]

I recognize the world is inundated with "Jacksploitation,"[4] but my sincere intent is to make Jack accessible in the spirit of his vernacular ministry.

To fulfil my promise, I am drawing attention to ten things that make Jack a unique person. Others might have chosen different characteristics and Jack's complexity makes that understandable. Over half a century after his death, numerous and larger books bear witness to the reality that we, as J.R.R. Tolkien, once commented, will "never get to the bottom of him."[5]

~1~

Ireland
● ●

Because of his relationship to Oxford and Cambridge, many people assume Jack was English, but he was always gladly and proudly Irish. Even in England, Jack surrounded himself with Irish friends and relished his Anglo-Irish life. For Jack, the Irish were the only people worth living and dying amongst. As an atheist, he even thanked the gods that he was Irish. He even once compared heaven to Oxford set in County Down. It was a love affair that never ended.

Ireland is a land shrouded in mystery, beauty, faërie, and romance; its enigmatic existence birthing a litany of world-famous writers.[6] Its mystique has historically generated the resplendent storytelling language that paints the kind of unseen worlds made famous by Jack, yet Ireland has been "slow to acclaim his greatness."[7] But we can't really know Jack without understanding his relationship to Ireland.[8]

Ireland influenced Jack in innumerable ways, one being his initial source of otherworldliness and his search for Joy. Family holidays spent in Ballycastle and Castlerock under the shadow of Mussenden Temple and Dunluce Castle may have served as the inspiration for Narnia's Cair Paravel and stirred a young boy's already burgeoning imagination. Its emerald green landscape carpets the borderland of Heaven in *The Great Divorce* and many of its natural wonders serve as significant features in Narnia, where Jack fulfilled his dream by placing a fictional population of his own choosing in Ireland.[9]

The green grass, lush unending rolling hills, awe-evoking mountains, eternal sea, and forever sky all inspired romanticism in Jack, who, like Shasta in *A Horse and His Boy*, quickly became a lifelong lover of northernness.[10] More than once, Jack commented that his early Irish life was his happiest and, until his father died in 1929, he returned often, even honeymooning there. For Jack, the end of school days in England was synonymous with Heaven and those holidays were always spent in Ireland.

Jack was born at home in one of two rented semidetached houses known as Dundela Villas in Strandtown, a suburb of Belfast. It was "the most economically successful city in Ireland… [and]…one of the leading industrial ports in Europe."[11] Jack visited the shipyard with his grandfather Richard who, at one time, had interests in its major shipbuilder. The harbor and sea provided him with a further sense of adventurous longing and the sound of a ship's horn always reminded him of his childhood. From both of his Irish homes, Jack looked north to the long mountain line of the Antrim Hills of which Cave Hill has two striking features: Belfast Castle and the profile of a sleeping giant's face.[12] His seemingly infinite horizon was filled with never-ending mountains, majestic castles, the mysterious Irish Sea, and on a clear day, far-off Scotland, all creating a realm in which it seemed that giants could rise to life at any moment.

From birth until death, Jack was always Irish. The island stirred his longing to be in a far-off country and inspired his imagination about it. The emerald isle made "him the boy that he was and the man that he ultimately became."[13] As such, there is a definite "connection between his first place and his final achievement…"[14] He is a reflection of the Ireland he loved and as such, it is one of the earliest of the cascading elements that made him unique. Ireland was Jack's secret country. It made him and then he remade it.

Think About It
....

Ireland has produced four Nobel laureates: W.B. Yeats (1923), George Bernard Shaw (1925), Samuel Beckett (1969) and Seamus Heaney (1995). Comparatively speaking, this is a substantial number of honorees for the island's population. On the fiftieth anniversary of his death, (22 November 2013), Jack, "one of Ireland's greatest sons,"[15] was honored with a memorial stone at Poet's Corner at Westminster Abbey.

~2~

Childhood

Born on 29 November 1898, Jack's father, Albert, was an attorney for the city of Belfast, from whom Jack inherited his rhetorical skills. His mother, Flora, was a homemaker and Queen's University honors graduate whose logical thinking enhanced Jack's naturally keen mind. Jack notes that his passion for other-worldliness came from neither parent. His brother, Warnie, was three years older. His Anglo-Irish childhood home, Ireland's Protestant-Catholic division, and the uncivil wars that horrifically divided the nation throughout his lifetime (among other things) gave him a dislike for politics and served to promote a *mere Christianity*[16] that united rather than divided Christians.[17]

Albert and Flora were married at and attended St. Mark's in Dundela (Church of Ireland) where their funerals were also held. Her father was its first rector and served the church during Jack's early life. He was baptized and confirmed there. Visiting his grandfather, young Jack encountered the face of a lion on the rectory's red door, perhaps an early model for Aslan. But as a child, Jack perceived religion as emotionally cold, intellectually stagnating, dutiful, impersonal, and without any sense of beauty, imagination, awe or Joy.

Within three years of his birth, Jack's parents employed Lizzie Endicott as his nursemaid, a woman in whom he could remember no fault and one of two blessings in his early childhood (the other being Warnie). It was she who initially introduced him to the world of myth and story, perhaps serving as a model for the nurse in *Prince Caspian* who dared whisper Aslan's name in the unsupernatural world of King Miraz.

When Jack was six, the family moved to Little Lea, a house Albert built and home to the Lewis men for twenty-five years. The house seemed as large as a city to the boys and they roamed every part of it, eventually settling down into a little end room in the attic where they created imaginary worlds.[18] Little Lea was a living character and major influence in Jack's life.[19] He was raised in a library of books that were literally everywhere, and everything was made available to his voracious reading appetite. The worlds inside and outside of Little Lea exhilarated Jack's imagination and multiplied his passion for otherworldliness. His cousin remembers how she and Warnie sat inside a wardrobe while Jack delighted them with stories of imaginary worlds.

The year before Jack's birth, typhoid affected 27,000 people in Belfast, its health issues a common symptom of late nineteenth century life. His parents mistakenly diagnosed him with a weak chest and kept him indoors as much as possible. But those long, dreary, wet days also fueled Jack's imagination and laid the foundation for his literary success. In addition, Belfast's "alarmingly high infant mortality rate"[20] and "the fear of having fevers such as typhoid during the warm summer months,"[21] motivated Flora and the boys to holiday away from Belfast for up to three months every year. Of course, the Lewis family travelled by horse-drawn carriage and train, and at least three of the Narnia stories—*The Horse and His Boy, The Voyage of the Dawn Treader* and *The Silver*

Chair—are set in the context of such a journey toward Aslan, perhaps reflective of Jack's own journey toward Christ.

Only a month after moving into Little Lea, Warnie returned to England for school, and Jack's days became increasingly solitary and imaginary. Albert, Warnie, and Jack all suffered from the lack of a joint closest to the hand in each thumb, disabling Jack's athletic abilities and discouraging participation in sports. But disability combined with Belfast's weather, his isolation from other boys, and summer holidays enjoyed at home (after he began school), drove him further into his imaginative world.

According to Ruth Pitter, a friend and poet, Jack lived for all of his life in "an almost uniquely persisting *child's* sense of glory and nightmare."[22] Before the end of the first chapter in *Surprised by Joy*, he vividly and painfully recalls one nightmare that forever shaped his life.

Think About It
·····························

Some people can't recall childhood. Others try to ignore, suppress or deny it. But no one escapes it. Jack retained his childhood feelings in his adult memories, enabling him to alchemize his suffering. His ability to retrieve those moments in meticulously raw detail enabled him to uniquely relate therapeutically to children and adults.

~3~

Death

Flora's death following surgery for abdominal cancer on 23 August 1908 was the painful chasm between Jack's childhood and boyhood.[23] He was nine. She was forty-six and died on Albert's forty-fifth birthday, only six days before their fourteenth wedding anniversary. Albert's grief was compounded by his father's death in April of that year. His brother, Joseph, died ten days after Flora. Albert tore the daily Shakespearean quote "Men must endure their going hence" from the family calendar and kept it the rest of his life. Warnie carved it into Jack's gravestone, a grave now occupied by Warnie as well. Flora's loss left Albert utterly, chronically bereaved and Jack felt he lost both parents in his mother's passing.[24]

Flora's death was preceded by her gradual

loss, a concept Jack later employed to describe the slow, torturous path to Hell, but it also compounded his longing and hope for other-worldliness.[25] She exchanged precious, treasured time with him for her sickbed, nurses, and doctors—strangers who turned his beloved Little Lea into a foreign world. A month later, Jack's diary records that he was reading *Paradise Lost*, no doubt feeling his own paradise to be lost as well.[26] He recalls that everything stable and reliable disappeared with his mother, like the greatest mythological city ever known, Atlantis and even whole continents sinking into the ocean. The impact of her death was incalculable, and he rarely spoke of it. In later life, a student once shared about the loss of his own mother, but Jack's response ensured the matter was never discussed again.[27] As late as 1953, he confessed that he still felt like a lost little boy with much of Flora remaining in him. But this was just the first life-changing death he experienced.

As a student at Oxford, Jack chose to support Britain's war effort and enlisted in Officer Training School.[28] The alphabet billeted him next to Edward Francis Courtney, "Paddy" Moore, who introduced eighteen-year-old

Jack to his separated but never divorced forty-five-year-old mother, Janie, and his eleven-year-old sister, Maureen. The Moores quickly became Jack's surrogate family and, as was not unusual for comrades in war, the two men covenanted to care for each other's family in the event that one of them died. Sadly, Paddy was among the approximately 35,000 Irishmen who died in the war that did not end all wars. And Jack kept his promise to Paddy.

Jack arrived at the front lines in France on his nineteenth birthday (29 November 1917) as a lieutenant with the First Somerset Light Infantry. He spent three weeks in February hospitalized for trench fever but soon returned to the war. On 15 April 1918, a British shell fell short of its intended target and shrapnel lodged in his left wrist, left leg, and upper left ribs, puncturing his left lung very close to his heart.[29] While convalescing in London, a depressed and homesick Jack wrote heartfelt letters begging his father to visit him, but Albert never did so. Jack then opted for a convalescent home near the Moores in Bristol. He was demobilized in December and returned to Oxford in January 1919 where he, Mrs. Moore, and Maureen lived in rented homes until they and Warnie pooled their money to buy the Kilns.[30]

Jack attempted to bury the horror of the war in the battleground alongside many friends and God. He rarely talked about his experiences and was quick to dismiss its dreadfulness, noting that he suffered greater in English boarding schools. Yet he also confessed that the war haunted him and gave him nightmares for many years. It also taught him to mistrust the twentieth century's hope in mechanization and technology as potential saviors, the war proving humanity incapable of managing such world-destroying power.

Flora's loss and the death of friends in the war permanently wounded Jack and forever framed his worldview. It initially reinforced his atheism but once he became a Christian, Jack saw himself in enemy-occupied territory and he assumed the identity of a saboteur fighting against the reigning secular worldview. Several letters in *The Screwtape Letters*, which Jack wrote during World War II, contain advice about the effect of war on the human soul.[31] Jack also placed much of *The Chronicles of Narnia* in the context of individual and global, physical and spiritual warfare. The Ransom Trilogy as well, reminds readers of the ceaseless, personal and cosmic battle between the contrasting ideologies of materialism and supernaturalism. In each, death is so much more than simply physical or temporal; it is dehumanizing, spiritual and eternal.

During WW II, the British Broadcasting Corporation enabled Jack to speak to the nation as a former soldier who understood death as well as the spiritually devastating effects of war. Those broadcasts made Jack a public intellectual; a lone, heroic, Christian, defiantly standing against what he perceived to be the "long defeat,"[32] of Western civilization as he knew it. Those broadcasts propelled him to even greater notoriety and added to the variegated circumstances that increased his popularity and influence.

Think About It
•••••••••••••••••••••••••••

The death of his mother and its resulting circumstances permanently altered the course of a young Jack's life. The death of Paddy, several friends, and innumerable other young lives in the trench warfare of WWI also dramatically transformed him. Death uniquely re-formed Jack's view of God, the world, ultimate reality, and his place in it—first as an atheist and then as a Christian.

~4~

Schools

Less than a month after Flora's death, Albert returned Warnie to Wynyard, his English boarding school, and sent nine-year-old Jack there also. Jack renamed the school Belsen after a German concentration camp.[33] Wynyard was a very small school, run by its founder, Robert "Oldie" Capron, an Anglican priest who had been privately declared insane two years earlier. Eleven days after his arrival, Jack wrote Albert the first of many letters begging to be released. His misery multiplied exponentially ten months later when Warnie moved on to Malvern College, leaving Jack to endure almost two horrific years under Oldie's lunacy. Not surprisingly, his chapter about Belsen is the longest in *Surprised by Joy*.

The school closed for a lack of students in

April 1910 and soon thereafter sixty-year-old Oldie died of pneumonia in an asylum. The only positive factor at Wynyard was Jack's attendance at an Anglo-Catholic church that re-animated his faith and where he first learned to fear Hell. Jack felt that Oldie's insanity made his cruelty forgivable, yet it was only months before his own death that Jack was able to forgive the first cruel man he ever encountered.

After the closing of Belsen, Jack returned home to Belfast where he attended Campbell College, only a few miles from Little Lea, but Albert removed him halfway through the term because of an illness. His experiences there were mostly positive, although he recalls one act of bullying. Yet he felt as if he didn't belong, enduring intense loneliness and the feeling of homelessness which he compared to living in a railway station as though always on the move.[34]

Albert returned Jack to England in January of 1911 to attend Cherbourg House, a preparatory school associated with Malvern, where Warnie was attending school.[35] Jack learned virtually nothing at Wynyard but maintained his faith. At Cherbourg, his education excelled, but he lost his faith. He became an atheist before his fourteenth birthday and, in correspondence, acknowledges that he was all too happy to abandon a God whom he deemed all too happy to condemn him to Hell.

In the Spring of 1913, Jack won a scholarship to Malvern, a school he renamed Wyvern in his autobiography so that he could vengefully criticize it.[36] By the time he arrived, just two months before his fifteenth birthday, Warnie had been dismissed for smoking, and Jack didn't enjoy the relational success of his older brother.[37] Malvern was run by "Bloods," a cultish fraternity of athletic upperclassmen who brutalized younger students. The "fagging," any duty assigned by a senior boy, was perpetual and exhausting. He hated the school and intentionally tried not to fit in, which only increased his isolation. He recalled this bullying in the Experiment House school attended by Eustace and Jill in *The Silver Chair*.

Jack's school experiences increased his pessimism and encouraged his atheism. Yet even Jack confesses that he was living a tormented existence between romanticism and rationalism (the spiritual and secular). Death taught him to detest this world and long for another, but seemingly perpetual unhappiness diminished any hope for it. He was angry at God for not existing and simultaneously angry at God for creating such a horrible world. But on holiday in April of 1914, he met Arthur Greeves, thereafter his closest friend and one who constantly encouraged him toward Christianity. Back at school, Jack made one final, desperate appeal to his father, threatening to shoot himself if Albert didn't rescue him.

Eustace and Jill escaped Experiment House through an almost-always locked door in a stone wall surrounding the school. Fifteen-year-old Jack fled Malvern for private tutoring with W.T. Kirkpatrick, a fellow Ulster Scot and former tutor for both Albert and Warnie. He arrived at Great Bookham less than three months after the start of World War I and quickly wrote to Arthur about his good fortune.[38] Jack remained there from 1914–1917 and dedicated an entire chapter of *Surprised by Joy* to 'the Great Knock" as the Lewis men referred to him, one of the most influential men in his life.[39]

He excelled at Great Bookham in many ways but not in Christianity. Kirkpatrick was a former Presbyterian seminary student turned atheist. Yet Jack ultimately saw Christianity as the rational end of Kirkpatrick's Socratic thinking; (God "knocking out" the Great Knock). It was also at Great Bookham that Jack encountered George MacDonald, who would also change his life, yet in an entirely different way.

Kirkpatrick prepared Jack for Oxford where he brilliantly earned a double first in Honors Moderations (Greek and Latin texts) and Greats (classical history and philosophy), and a first in English language and literature, graduating for that degree in one year instead of the normal three.[40] He taught philosophy for one year and, in 1925, became a fellow and tutor in English literature at Magdalen College, holding that position until he became the first professor of Medieval and Renaissance Literature at Cambridge from 1954 until 1963 when he retired for health reasons.[41]

It was at Oxford that Jack encountered life-altering relationships with Christians who were intellectually capable of successfully challenging his atheism. Although most famous for his Christian writing, Jack was a leading scholar in Medieval and Renaissance literature and highly respected in academia, several of his scholarly works still authoritative. But Jack's willingness to publish popular theology in fiction was one of the reasons that Oxford elites criticized and ostracized him.[42] This hurt him personally, Jack once describing himself as a hated man, and the hostility cost him professionally.[43] He nonetheless continued to serve as a public intellectual, engaging the world at what he perceived to be its greatest need—spiritual amnesia.

Jack became a Christian at Oxford and there, as well as at Cambridge, his humor, rhetoric, former atheism, blue-collar presentations of Christianity, and sincere passion for students made him the most popular lecturer, influencing a generation of irreligious but spiritually hungry people.

Think About It

Jack's particular experiences in English boarding schools initially affected him negatively but those dark memories dawned into a horizon of hope for the children who read *The Chronicles of Narnia*. His life was, once again, radically and permanently altered when he became a Christian at Oxford. Cambridge honored him with a professorship when that "other" University refused to do so. Each school in Jack's life contributed to his uniqueness as an adult and author.

~5~

Joy
• •

Jack's first encounter with other-world epiphanies was the memory of an incident that occurred at Dundela Villas. It wasn't the actual event but the memory of it that first swept him into unknown worlds. As Jack stood beside a flowering currant bush at Little Lea, he remembered a miniature garden of grass, sticks, and moss that Warnie had brought into his nursery from their garden. The experience lasted only a moment and was gone almost before he really knew it was happening but it overwhelmed him with a sense of desire so strong that nothing in his young life compared to it. The second experience occurred when he was reading *Squirrel Nutkin*, a book by one of his favorite childhood authors, Beatrix Potter, and he was overwhelmed with the sense of Autumn. Later, when reading from the English translation of the Swedish poem, *Drapa*, he was suddenly transported into the cold and immense world of "northernness" and then quickly returned with the same forceful, sickening rapidity.

According to Jack, these three experiences are central to his life story, outlining its whole progression. His existence has no meaning apart from them, nor can his life be understood without them. Even before he was six years old, such experiences defined longing and beauty for him. He uses the German word *Sehnsucht* to explain this painful, yet pleasurable, intense feeling of exile and alienation simultaneously coupled with the longing or desire for the transcendent, unnamed, unknown of the soul's true home. It was, for him, "a foretaste of ultimate reality."[44] This "Joy was something he wanted permanently, and he wanted it more than anything else."[45]

Jack lived an exiled life after the death of Flora. The nightmare of Oldie increased his longing to escape, to escape even this world. But those two horrific experiences also demolished any hope of Joy. Apart from the Anglo-Catholic church, the only other good thing was that Belsen taught him to live by faith, looking forward to holidays in the same way that Christians hope for Heaven. Cherbourg demolished Jack's faith but while he was there, his passion for Joy was reanimated when one bright shadow of Joy dawned on Jack's pessimistic, discouraged, materialistic world and awakened him from his spiritual slumber.

While reading the magazine *Bookman*, Jack saw a headline titled "Siegfried and the Twilight of the Gods" with an illustration by Arthur Rackham.[46] He was, once more, immediately consumed by Northernness, swept away into that all-desired, yet unidentifiable region of the vast, mysterious unknown and then returned with equal lightning speed. During his next holiday home in Belfast, Jack stood in a record shop and heard Wagner's *Ride of the Valkyries*, an opera with which he was thereafter enamored. That summer he found the book *Siegfried and the Twilight of the Gods* with Rackham's illustrations in the home of his cousin. Not since his childhood at Little Lea had he experienced such emotional upheaval. It made everything else in his life of second importance. For Jack, his long joyless winter had passed. His quest for Joy reanimated a new romantic Spring. It was the same kind of overwhelming, life-altering emotion felt by the Pevensies children when they first heard the name of Aslan whispered by Mr. Beaver.

These discoveries of such beauty and wonder, however, caused a conundrum. Now a young atheist, his rationalism denied the supernatural, but his romantic longings desired it. Dare he hope? Dare he believe? This problem moved him to live in two contrasting worlds: one, his internal, mental world of beauty and spirituality; the other, his physical, external world of school and materialism.

Jack later discovered that Christianity is both rational and romantic, explaining and expressing both worlds. He also understood that God used his passion for *Sehnsucht,* Norse mythology, and Joy as precursors to faith in Christ, shadows of the true light, signposts pointing toward Christ, the ultimate Reality. And he employed it all, pagan and Christian, to uniquely imagine stories that continue to enthuse hearts with the Joy he found in Jesus.

Think About It

·····························

The title of Jack's autobiography is taken from William Wordsworth's elegy to his three-year old deceased daughter, Catherine. In it, Wordsworth describes the guilt and sorrow that he felt for an unexpected, but short-lived moment of Joy that was immediately interrupted by the memory of her loss and his inability to share that happiness with her. Jack's Joy was also initially fleeting, but he eventually discovered that all lesser and temporary Joys point to Jesus as their ultimate and permanent reality.

~6~

Atheism

At Cherbourg, Jack encountered intelligent, atheistic teachers who actively campaigned against Christianity and introduced him to a rationale for unbelief.[47] He also met "Miss Cowie," the spiritually seeking but immature young matron of the school, whom Jack undoubtedly looked to as a mother figure.[48] Unaware of his internal battle between rationalism and romanticism or of his lifelong passion for the preternatural, Miss Cowie unintentionally introduced Jack to the occult and mysticism, a path to spirituality without God.

Cherbourg's influence catapulted him away from the stern Christianity he already disdained, as well as the unwanted, divine judgement that accompanied such belief. At thirteen,

Jack abandoned his childhood faith and gladly embraced a life without God and the fear of Hell. After Cherbourg, Jack believed in no religion. He challenged those who disagreed with him and argued that, if there was any reason for religion, Christianity would be the worst representation of the God who was not there.

After Malvern, Jack's tenure with Kirkpatrick reinforced his atheism. He arrived at Gastons,[49] maintaining that inconsistent, illogical anger toward God for not existing but also for creating such a fallen world. That conflict, as well as the fear of his father, drove him, four months later, to commit what he considered one of the most cowardly and hypocritical acts of his life—confirmation in the Anglican church during the Christmas holiday of 1914.

Jack considered Kirkpatrick to be the nearest thing to a purely logical entity he ever experienced and the only person who referred to Jack as Clive. For three years, Kirkpatrick tutored Jack in logic and rationalistic philosophy, impressed intellectual integrity upon him, and framed Jack's passion for medieval scholarship while honing his ability in languages, even predicting Jack's potential occupation as an author and academic. Paradoxically, it was Kirkpatrick's mandate for consistent logic that caused an intellectually honest Jack to eventually, although reluctantly, accept Theism, then embrace Christianity and defend it with the logical rigor of *Mere Christianity*.

Jack was always an uncomfortable, conflicted atheist and never a quiet one. By the time he returned from the war, he was a hurt, angry young activist. His flagrant disdain for God went public with his first book, a collection of overtly dark poems titled, *Spirits in Bondage* (1919). Written in the despairing cynicism that characterized much of the post-World War I generation, the book describes a God who malevolently opposes his creation with death as the ultimate Victor.

Even though it was published under the pseudonym of Clive Hamilton (his first name and his mother's maiden name), Albert was embarrassed by it and angry with Jack for potentially jeopardizing any future career with such public anti-God rhetoric. Warnie assured his father that Jack's sentiment was only a passing fad, but history proves it was not. Jack was a sincere and serious atheist for approximately twenty formative years of his life and the book represents Jack's passionate commitment to atheism. He would later embrace Christianity with the same private vigor and public transparency.

Think About It

....

Jack's unbelief found its ultimate target in the Christian God who epitomized the supernatural or otherworldliness. In time, it became easier to completely deny the existence of the Joy he sometimes experienced, especially when contrasted with the almost-constant sorrow he endured. Cherbourg presented him with spiritual alternatives to Christianity and he discovered a logical rationale for unbelief at Great Bookham. But at Oxford, Jack encountered both romantic and rational challenges to his skepticism.

~7~

Conversion

Jack's sole purpose in writing *Surprised by Joy* was to narrate his conversion from atheism to Christianity and the particular place of Joy in his spiritual journey. His initial argument against God was moral, not intellectual, and the reasons were multiple. God had failed to protect his mother, rescue him from Oldie, provide him with friends, and save him from the relentless rollercoaster of prepubescent emotions. World War I exponentially multiplied his tenaciously held position. There was simply no reason for God to exist, and if he did, he shouldn't.

Life's circumstances made Jack doubt, even detest his early, other-world experiences, and he intentionally set them aside. It was better not to hope. But living in a secular world didn't satisfy him either. It was too simplistic and unfulfilling. He re-experienced *Joy* at Cherbourg but influences there moved him away from Christian spirituality. The romantic and rational sides of his brain fought for supremacy as he strove within himself to find a world in which neither passion had to be excluded and both loves might unite in peace and happiness. After Cherbourg, Jack sincerely engaged in myriad philosophical perspectives in his vigorous attempt to evade the divine Interferer. His diary, letters, and autobiography all demonstrate that painful, tumultuous process.

On 4 March 1916, after a long, afternoon walk, Jack opted to take the train back to Great Bookham. As he stood on the empty platform, he visited the bookstall, discovering a copy of George McDonald's *Phantastes*. Jack's world was revolutionized by it, a watershed moment that immersed him in a fantastical world of otherness that he could not and no longer desired to deny. However, MacDonald's otherworldliness was different from anything Jack had previously encountered. Instead of leaving his realm, the supernatural invaded and transformed his world – the light entered his darkness - with something that he later understood to be the holiness of Christianity.

Jack left Great Bookham for Oxford in 1917 and endured a long, excruciating and incremental return to Christianity. Although his atheism had begun with a moral argument against God, it ended when he could no longer maintain an honest intellectual war against Christianity. At Oxford he encountered Christians like Nevil Coghill, whom Jack thought to be brilliant in spite of his Christianity. Owen Barfield made him doubt Kirkpatrick's philosophical realism. All of his reading turned against him; the books he liked best were written by Christians. One evening, the philosopher T.D. Weldon, whom Jack thought to be the toughest atheist he ever knew, sat in Jack's room by a late-night fire and acknowledged the resurrection of Jesus. His words shook Jack to the core. J.R.R. Tolkien and Hugo Dyson walked patiently alongside him until he understood the pagan myths he loved and the story of a dying god in particular, were all about the incarnated Christ who is the foundational, unique, true and ultimate myth.[50]

Jack fought hard not to acknowledge the personal God of Christianity, but he eventually became convinced of the existence of an Absolute. One early June night of 1930, he knelt in his room at Magdalen College in Oxford and reluctantly surrendered to the God of theism. Eventually, however, Jack could not argue with the evidence for Jesus and Christianity. On 28 September 1931, he stepped into the sidecar of Warnie's motorcycle for a family visit to the Whipsnade Zoo.[51] When Jack began the trip, he was not a Christian and when he got out of the sidecar, he was. It was that simple. It was that certain. It was that monumental. He was two months shy of his thirty-third birthday.

Think About It

....

Jack's war between the natural and supernatural is metaphorically reflected in the battle between winter and spring in *The Lion, the Witch and the Wardrobe.* But Christianity offered him a comprehensive narrative for all of reality and it satisfied him intellectually, spiritually, and emotionally. He could not honestly ignore or intellectually deny it. Thereafter, he devoted his entire life to explaining and defending Christianity through the lens of his unique, whole-life conversion.

~8~

People

There is a sense in which Jack can be defined by the people in his life. Friendship was so important to him that he sought it out, worked hard to maintain it, thoroughly enjoyed it, and greatly benefited from it. He loved traipsing through the woods with friends, sitting by a fire drinking beer, and smoking pipes. He is famous for his barrel laugh. Jack wrote a book (*The Four Loves*) in which he devoted a chapter to the love between friends and even defined Heaven as the resurrection of those friendships enjoyed on earth. He dedicated *The Problem of Pain* to the Inklings who proved an antidote for his essentially friendless boyhood. He thought of friendship as something angelic, able to give mortals some sense of what it means to be a god. Here is just a glimpse of some of the most important people in Jack's life.

Only four of Arthur Greeves' letters to Jack are known to exist, but Arthur kept most of Jack's letters. They lived on the same street in Belfast and were both fifteen when their mutual passion for Norse mythology created their lasting friendship. There were periods of his life when no one knew Jack better than Arthur, who taught him charity and whom Jack failed to teach arrogance. On 11 September 1963, only two months before his death, Jack completed his last letter to his lifelong friend with the words "But oh Arthur, never to see you again!"[52]

Jack labored to keep his life at the Kilns very private from his academic world, but his view of friendship helps explain his commitment to Paddy, whose mother he lived with longer than any other woman. There is unending speculation about his relationship to Mrs. Moore. Maureen evidently told two biographers (George Sayer and A.N. Wilson) that it was initially intimate. Regardless, Jack eventually came to view her as a surrogate mother and the person who taught him kindness. He hid their connection from Albert for as long as he could. Warnie never liked her. It strained his association with multiple others. Still, they lived together until the last nine months of her life and when her dementia required confinement to a nursing home, Jack visited her almost daily. Yet even he reflected differently on the relationship after Mrs. Moore died.[53]

Jack's friendship with fellow medievalist, John Ronald Reuel Tolkien, was legendary.[54] The two men met first at a faculty meeting on 11 May 1926 and soon thereafter met weekly, usually on Mondays, a possible precursor to the Inklings. Tolkien's perspective on myth and the dying god was instrumental in Jack's conversion. He credited Lewis's encouragement with the completion and publication of *The Hobbit* and *The Lord of the Rings.* Still, Tolkien didn't care for *The Chronicles of Narnia*; its mixing of mythologies and its obvious Christianity. Their relationship cooled around 1940, yet the two always held each other in high esteem: Jack dedicating *The Screwtape Letters* to Tolkien (1942) and Tollers, as he was affectionately known, recommending Jack to the newly created chair of Chair of Medieval and Renaissance Literature at Cambridge (1954).

Charles Williams and Jack exchanged mutual fan letters in 1936. They met in London in 1938 and became good friends when the Oxford Press moved Williams to Oxford in 1940 in order escape the German blitzkrieg of London. Like Jack, he was a committed Anglican, but, unlike Jack, dabbled in the occult. Even though they knew each other for only five years, Jack stated that Charles had influenced his writing more than any other.[55] Williams died while preparing to move back to London and Jack was deeply affected. He expressed his feelings through numerous letters, wrote a short poem, and helped secure his friend's literacy legacy.

The Inklings are one of the most famous literary groups in history. Their name was borrowed from a defunct Oxford literary society and has perhaps three connotations: those who use ink to write, who have only an inkling of what they will write about when they start, and who possess an inkling of a supernatural and future world. With Jack at the center, these friends and provocateurs met in his rooms at Magdalen College every Thursday evening when school was in session. That fellowship spilled over into an informal gathering each Tuesday morning at a pub called "The Eagle and the Child," known to locals as "Bird and Baby."

This eclectic group met from the early 1930s

until the late 1940s and whether on Tuesday or Thursday, varied in number of attendees, depending on each man's availability. Tuesday was an informal, public meeting of conversation, laughter, pipes and beer but Thursday evenings were more serious and by invitation only. There was no prearranged agenda, but the gathering normally began around nine with Jack putting on tea and asking if someone had anything to read. As such, the Inklings was a literary reading group and yet, in spontaneous concert with likeminded others who were never part of their group, they formed a collective of intellectuals who were intent on redeeming Western civilization.[56]

Jack played a pivotal role in the Christian conversion of American Marxist atheists, William and Helen Joy Davidman Gresham. They began corresponding while she was still in a troubled marriage and living in the USA. Joy visited England and met Jack in 1952, returned home and then went back to England in late 1953. Her divorce became final in August of the next year and Jack, sixteen years her elder, married Joy in a civil ceremony on 23 April 1956 in a sympathetic effort to help her avoid deportation. Six months later, she was diagnosed with terminal cancer and Jack was truly surprised by his love for Joy. Jack again married Joy on 21 March 1957 in a bed-side, Anglican service and then adopted her two sons, David and Douglas, to whom he dedicated *The Horse and His Boy*. Joy's influence on Jack is inestimable and her death on 13 July 1960, that of the third woman Jack loved, moved him to write the very intimate, *A Grief Observed*, initially published under the pseudonym of N.W. Clerk[57] but in his real name after Jack's death.[58]

Friendships made Jack, and this chapter does not do justice to any of those mentioned. Nor does it speak to the myriad other people who positively or negatively influenced him, or of the many friendships he held dear. But friendship is another essential aspect of what made Jack a unique person and, to know him, it is important to know his friends.

Think About It

People were extremely important to Jack. From his perspective, friendship gave meaning to his existence and made him human. Each friendship brings out something unique in every friend and, as a result, enhances each and the whole group of friends; hence, the more, the merrier! Friendships aren't created by looking at each other but together looking at something of mutual interest, something of such importance and meaning that it binds hearts. Such friendships change people (they certainly did so for Jack) and can potentially change the world.

~9~

Romantic Apologetics

When Jack became a Christian in 1931, he had already anonymously published two books, one of poetry and the other a narrative poem[59], and was working on his first academic book, *The Allegory of Love* (1936). In the interim, Jack went public with his faith in his first fiction prose, *The Pilgrim's Regress: An Allegorical Apology for Christianity, Reason and Romanticism* (1933) a novel written in less than two weeks while on summer holiday with Arthur Greeves, and dedicated to his dear friend.[60] *Regress* was Jack's first attempt to "spin a tale that would envelop his readers in an imaginative web nearly against their will, cast a spell that would rekindle, reignite a longing that dared not speak its name, a longing for home, what Jack called 'the true east.'"[61]

His next novel, *Out of the Silent Planet* (1938), outlines the basic storyline of Scripture: creation, sin, fall, and redemption. He intended the Ransom Trilogy[62] to counter the non-Christian worldview of scientism[63] found in works like those of H.G. Wells, which he enjoyed as a young boy.[64]

Ashley Sampson, the editor for a Christian book series, recognized the romantic orthodoxy in *Out of the Silent Planet* and asked Jack to write a volume on suffering. In the preface to that book, his first nonfiction apologetic for Christianity, *The Problem of Pain* (1940), Jack acknowledges that he wrote the book to help unbelievers better understand what Christians believe and their reasons for doing so. The very next year (and as a direct result of reading that book) J.W. Welch, director of the British Broadcasting Corporation, asked Jack to provide a series of broadcast talks for the nation once again at war and in need of divine hope. That four-part series, heard over the revolutionary invention of radio, made Jack a household name, provided him with an unprecedented, diverse audience, and produced *Mere Christianity*, one of the most influential apologetic books of the twentieth century.[65] *The Screw-*

tape Letters (1942) earned him the cover of *Time* Magazine in 1947.[66]

Jack asserted that he did not write as a formally educated theologian.[67] But he also thought the British clergy had misrepresented Christianity with heartless, unimaginative, unintelligible explanations of the gospel. The Church had missed the reality that reason comprehends truth, but imagination gives it meaning. What Christianity needed most was a translator, a smuggler, someone who, more than informing people, simply reminded them of what is true. So, he took Christianity out of its traditional, stained-glass, high church intellectualism and reimagined it in the accessible vernacular of the average layperson. He did not intend to argue people into Christianity. Instead, he hoped to bypass the kind of preconceived arguments that hindered his faith. He remythologized truth in a metaphorical style of imaginative evangelism. That spiritual subterfuge finds its most famous megaphone in *The Chronicles of Narnia*.[68]

Jack was also not afraid of paganism and this, combined with his Christianity, provides him with a distinct worldview. For all his life, he loved the mysterious unknown of northernness, Norse mythology, and pagan stories. For him, paganism is unfinished Christianity, stories with incomplete Christ-figures who point to Jesus as their ultimate reality. It was his love of these myths that initially caught his attention and then enraptured him with the true myth made historical fact in the incarnation of Jesus. These fragments of the truth were not stumbling blocks to his faith, but the path to it, and so he generously employed them in his writing.

For most of his life, Jack lived in a supernatural world. As a Christian, he created realms that stirred the imagination and engaged the reason, something to look into and through, out of this world and into another, but expressly for the purpose of returning back into this world as a changed person and then looking on, to the next. His fiction works aren't escapism but exactly the opposite: a sign post or a wardrobe door to the true reality. His childhood experiences with *Sehnsucht* provided him with the basis of longing for Heaven. The Anglo-Catholic church at Belsen taught him to fear Hell. In a world created and governed by a supernatural God, Heaven and Hell were facts for Jack. And he firmly believed that we are, every moment of our lives, willfully choosing one or the other as our final, ultimate, irreconcilable destination. It is this unique, rationally romantic apologetic expressed in myriad genres that secures Jack's ever-increasing, global influence.

Think About It

Jack leveraged his position as an academic and religious outsider to appeal to a wide and vast audience. Focusing on mere Christianity enabled otherwise differing people to assemble around his central ideas. Writing in multiple genres only increased the potential conveyance of his universal truth to a diverse population. He deconstructed what people thought they knew about Christianity and reconstructed it in the fantasy fiction of literary apologetics. Attracting the imagination first and then appealing to the intellect—reaching the whole person—he uniquely reached others as he had been reached.

~10~

Eschatology

Jack grew to believe in God in just the way he believed in the sun, seeing everything by God who illumines all of life. For him, every human desire has a corresponding satisfaction—either natural and temporal or supernatural and eternal. But all desire is really intended to do one thing: awaken this ultimate passion for an infinite Joy. If we discover a desire that cannot be naturally satisfied, it only proves we were made for another, supernatural world. Awakening this desire is an important step in directing people toward God and Jack intended to use every means possible to do so.

Jack's passion for Joy found its ultimate source and definition in Jesus, its final resting place in Heaven. He longed for Heaven and was very disappointed when his recovery from a heart attack delayed his entrance into that far-off country. Glory outweighed life and its importance weighed heavily on him personally and in his work. Jack knew that he was made for an eternal world and never settled for this temporal mud-puddled existence. He knew what it meant to vacation at the sea, longed for that pure, eternal ocean, and encouraged others to do the same. Jack was no half-hearted Christian. Only infinite Joy would satisfy him. And his heavenly-mindedness made him of the earthliest good.

World War I diminished Britain's religious hope, with post-war England seeking salvation in the nondivine. But Jack had personally experienced the horror that such modernity cruelly unleashed on the world, illustrating it, for instance, in the Ransom Trilogy—the villain in each book being a scientist.[69] As a medieval scholar, Jack also understood the powerful moral persuasion of the supernatural. Heaven and Hell are not simply eschatological concepts but personal and world-changing doctrines—matters of eternal life or death.

And so, Jack became adept at mythologizing the true and at fictionalizing the real, in an effort to capture the imagination of the religiously uneducated, indifferent or antagonistic masses. He was also very concerned about future generations educated on a secular, unsupernatural diet. He employed scenes like the Underland capture of Eustace and Jill (*The Silver Chair*) to demonstrate the spiritual battle between a kingdom of supernatural light and the dark sorrow of a materialist world.

Jack was also not satisfied to go to Heaven alone. His life before Christ demonstrated that not all who wonder are found, and he longed to share his spiritual journey into the truest story with fellow pilgrims. It became his mission to awaken and direct the awe that is resident within all of us. This was no trivial matter for him; it was eternal life or everlasting death.

Jack viewed no one as simply mortal. Everyone is immortal. Every moment moves us toward one of two eternal destinations, ultimately making us the person we will be forever. We are also influencing each other toward one of these two permanent ends. Jack attempted to describe the wonder of Heaven and the horror of Hell, but he also believed that each is beyond human comprehension. Heaven is too glorious; Hell is too terrible. Hell hallows us while Heaven gives us substance. Heaven makes us fully human; Hell makes us inhuman.

According to Jack, the longing for Heaven is an innate, fundamental desire. Nothing can do for us what only God in Heaven can do. Every person is haunted by a paradise-shaped hole that he alone can fill. In desire, God has woven into our being the only magical spell that can break the evil enchantment of this world. For now, we on the wrong side of the wardrobe door but we will one day step into that bright land without shadows.

But Heaven is just one of two ultimate and eternal destinations. Jack also believed in a literal, eternal Hell. Even though he personally detested the doctrine and wished it did not exist, he recognized that Jesus taught its undeniable reality. Some people are frustrated by Jack's lack of specificity concerning the nature of Hell but Jack thought that the awfulness of Hell was ultimately undefinable, too specific for words. Rather than attempt to define the nature of Hell, he invested his energy in warnings about it. Those who choose to embrace evil, as illustrated in *The Screwtape Letters*, endure Hell's self-annihilating effects. *The Great Divorce* masterfully demonstrates Jack's concept of a slow, willful, egotistical slide into unreprieveable Hell. The soul that consumes all other loves is eventually itself consumed. Eustace Scrubb illustrates the self-destructive journey to dragoness (*The Voyage of the Dawn Treader*) while Weston demonstrates the inhumanity of the walking dead (*Perelandra*).

For Jack, Hell is all about choice. We make our temporal choices until our choices eternally make us. The soul bound for Hell simultaneously rejects God and curves in on itself, so much so that Hell is unsurprising for its inhabitants. This makes Hell the consequence of choice, with only self to blame. Everyone gets the eternity most desired. Hell exists for successful revolutionaries who will not—cannot—change their minds. Cosmically speaking, Hell is a divine mercy, a tourniquet for evil.

Jack's death was overshadowed by the deaths of President John F. Kennedy and Aldous Huxley who both died on the same day. The world was so caught off guard that only eight people attended his funeral. Warnie was too distraught and inebriated, so Douglas Gresham represented the family. But Jack's comprehensive eschatological worldview—a perspective rooted in the past, fighting for the present and hoping for the future—speaks to the eternity within each of us, ensuring that "While Huxley is now largely forgotten and Kennedy remains a symbol of lost promise, Lewis lives on…"[70] and his influence grows with each passing year.

Think About It

Jack was an eschatological man. Heaven and Hell were of the greatest concern to him and these all-important themes can be found throughout his Christian writing. Although Hell was of equal importance to him, he is perhaps more famous for his depictions of Heaven. If his own life experiences were any indication, he knew that words are insufficient to describe the bliss of Heaven or the bane of Hell. He nonetheless employed his unique intellect and imagination in the evangelistic task of speaking of both Heaven and Hell.

Conclusion

Jack sincerely believed he would be forgotten five years after his death, but he was astoundingly wrong. Almost two decades into the twenty-first century, his books sell at a steady rate and his influence is increasing globally. As late as 7 August 2019, *The Lion, the Witch and the Wardrobe* was voted the most popular and favorite book in the United Kingdom

He survived his own battles, two world wars, and their consequences. The times made him and then God remade him. The resulting life recognized and spoke to the truest needs of any generation. His passionate, intellectual, imaginative, and Christian response to the world around him has granted him unparalleled influence in two different centuries.

Human beings are created in the image of God. This means that biography is a sacred task. This book has been undertaken with that understanding. Jack was a unique gift from God and for many reasons, ten of which have been noted in this book, he remains so. There will never be another Clive Staples Lewis. There doesn't need to be. Jack's God remains.

P.S. If you would like to talk more about Jack, e-mail me at reggieweems@gmail.com.

About the Author

REGGIE WEEMS is married to his childhood sweetheart, Teana. They share three children and ten grandchildren. He has pastored two congregations: the first for ten years and the second since 1991. He also teaches theology, Bible, and humanities at two universities and serves a Doctor of Ministry mentor. His DMin in Pastoral Leadership and Management is from Liberty University in Lynchburg, Virginia (USA), and his PhD in Historical Theology is from the University of Babes-Bolyai in Cluj-Napoca, Romania.

www.10thingsabout.org

To buy quantities of this book at a special rate for bulk use, email
info@greatwriting.org

Acknowledgments

The world of C.S. Lewis is one of many friendships, some of whom have been invaluable to this book.

Arthur Strong took the cover photograph. His daughter and my new friend, Ingrid Franzon, was kind enough to share the picture and its story, a treasure in and of itself.

Crystal Hurd reviewed the manuscript and offered critical assistance. I am extremely grateful for her friendship and expertise.

Sandy Smith, who intimately knows Jack's Ireland, also read the manuscript and offered valuable insight for which I am very thankful.

Endnotes

1 "Don v. Devil," *Time Magazine*. Monday, September 8, 1947. http://content.time.com/time/subscriber/article/0,33009,804196,00.html (accessed, 17 January 2019).

2 As a child, Lewis nicknamed himself 'Jacksie' and was thereafter called 'Jack' by family and friends.

3 Jack's popularity is exponential, in part because he wrote in multiple genres: academic literature and criticism, science fiction, fantasy, satire, nonfiction essays, autobiography; theology, philosophy, poetry, children's literature and Christian apologetics.

4 (Robert McSwain. "Introduction," *Cambridge Companion to C.S. Lewis*, ed., Robert McSwain and Michael Ward (Cambridge University Press, 2010), 11.

5 George Sayer. *Jack: A Life of C.S. Lewis* (Wheaton: Crossway Books, 1988, 1994), xvii.

6 Faërie is not the world of fairies. It is a mythological world beyond human experience. Romance is synonymous with the imaginative or mythical. Jack defined it as "Joy" in the 3rd edition of

The Pilgrim's Regress.

7 David Bleakley. *C.S. Lewis: At Home in Ireland* (Belfast: Strandtown Press, 1998), 14.

8 For an in-depth look at Jack's Ireland, consider reading *C.S. Lewis and the Island of His Birth: The Places, The Stories, The Inspiration,* by Alexander Smith.

9 For instance, the Cloughmore Stone, a 50-ton granite boulder located about 1000 feet above the village of Rostrevor in the Mourne Mountains and overlooking the Carlingford Lough in County Down may have served as Jack's inspiration for Aslan's table.

10 Northernness is a term Jack used to describe the numinous or utter other, a world of beauty and terror.

11 Ronald W. Bresland. *The Backward Glance: C.S. Lewis and Ireland* (Belfast: The Institute of Irish Studies, 1999), 17.

12 That profile is the suspected inspiration for Jonathan Swift's *Gulliver's Travels*, a favorite book of Jack's childhood.

13 Bleakley, *C.S. Lewis,* 15.

14 Ibid., 23.

15 Bleakley, 26.

16 The Puritan clergyman, Richard Baxter (1516-1691) coined the term *"meer Christianity."*

17 Consistent with his commitment to Christianity above politics, Jack declined the offer of CBE (Commander of the Order of the British Empire) or knighthood, concerned that the honor could

be misunderstood by those who saw religion as politically entrenched. For instance, in his 27 October 1944, *Tribune* review of *Beyond Personality*, George Orwell accused Jack of participating in a "big [political] counter-attack against the Left…" http://www.telelib.com/authors/O/OrwellGeorge/essay/tribune/AsIPlease19441027.html (accessed June 5, 2019).

18 Those stories have been posthumously published in a book now available as *Boxen: Childhood Chronicles Before Narnia.*

19 Jack transformed his Little Lea childhood home into the Oxford home of Professor Digory Kirke. Kirk is the Scottish word for Church, where Jack found sanctuary, much like the Pevensies children found refuge with Professor Kirke—all modeled after the real-life circumstance when children stayed with Jack during the WWII blitzkrieg on London.

20 Sayer, *Jack*, 39.

21 Richard V. James. "C.S. Lewis's Belfast Childhood" in *An Examined Life: C.S. Lewis Life, Works and Legacy*, Volume 1, ed., Bruce Edwards (Westport: Praeger, 2007), 1.

22 Donald E. Glover. *C.S. Lewis and the Art of Enchantment* (Athens: Ohio UP, 1981), 34.

23 I am proposing that Jack's childhood ended with Flora's death and began a boyhood that lasted until he entered Oxford.

24 Jack endured a strained relationship with Albert until weeks before his father's death. Albert may have reminded Jack of his lost childhood. After their father

died, Warnie and Jack buried their childhood toys in the yard of Little Lea, perhaps giving closure to their childhood. Jack later considered his ill treatment of his father to be his greatest sin.

25 Jack rewrote Flora's loss when Digory Kirke saved his mother from death in *The Magician's Nephew*, a book he was writing at the same time he wrote his autobiography, *Surprised by Joy*, in which he recalled the death of his mother.

26 Jack thought a good book was worth re-reading and he was still reading *Paradise Lost* the year he died.

27 Bleakley, *C.S. Lewis*, 57.

28 There was no conscription in Ireland which means that Irish citizens volunteered for World War I.

29 The fragments near his heart were not removed until 1944.

30 The Kilns was originally the site of two brick kilns. The typically English cottage was built in 1922 on an eight-acre plot and bought in 1930 under Mrs. Moore's name. It was Jack's home until he died in 1963.

31 *The Guardian* (1846-1951) was a weekly Anglican newspaper that originally published the 31 "Screwtape Letters" in weekly installments in 1941 and the book was published in February 1942.

32 The "long defeat" is an anti-modern term created by Tolkien to describe the noble but unwinnable war of worldviews that will require divine intervention for its ultimate victory. J.R.R. Tolkien, "Letter to Amy Ronald," 15 December 1956 in Humphrey Carpenter

& Christopher Tolkien. *The Letters of J.R.R. Tolkien*, (Wilmington: Mariner Books, 1981), 255.

33 Jack began school at Wynyard in September 1908.

34 The Pevensies children were never homeless but endured the same sort of transient existence between two worlds.

35 Jack started at Cherbourg in January 1911 and renamed the school Chartres in his autobiography.

36 A wyvern is a dragon with a diamond- or arrow-shaped tip for its tail.

37 Jack began school at Malvern on 18 September 1913. Eight days earlier, Warnie arrived at Great Bookham to study with W.T. Kirkpatrick. He then entered Sandhurst, a Royal Military Academy, on 4 February 1914.

38 Jack arrived at Great Bookham on 19 September 1914. Only about twenty-five miles from London, Jack could see the fires in London caused by Zeppelin bombings. Great Bookham was affected in many ways by the war—returning wounded veterans, housing refugees, etc. In response, Jack created a mental contract with the world in which he could ignore the war until he joined the British army.

39 Jack honored Kirkpatrick in the person of Digory Kirke.

40 Jack earned these degrees in 1920, 1922 and 1923.

41 Jack delivered his inaugural address on 29 November 1954, his fifty-sixth birthday, assumed the position in January of 1955, and was elected a Fellow of the British Academy in July of that same year.

42 Jack did so in *The Ransom Trilogy* (1938, 43, 45), *The Screwtape Letters* (1942), *The Great Divorce* (1945) and *The Chronicles of Narnia* (1950-56).

43 On more than one occasion, Oxford's animosity vetoed Jack's opportunity for professorships and even though it was painful, he had grown accustomed to living as an outsider in English schools.

44 Colin Duriez. "The Romantic Writer: Lewis's Theology of Fantasy," in *The Pilgrim's Guide: C.S. Lewis and the Art of Witness*, ed., David Mills (Grand Rapids: William B. Eerdmans Publishing Company, 1998), 105.

45 Perry C. Bramlett. "Lewis the Reluctant Convert: Surprised by Faith," in *An Examined Life: C.S. Lewis Life, Works and Legacy*, ed., Bruce L. Edwards (Westport: Praeger, 2007), 84-85.

46 Jack was reading the Christmas 1911 issue in May of 1912.

47 Jack attended Wynyard (Belsen), Campbell College, Cherbourg (Chartres), Malvern (Wyvern), Great Bookham and Oxford.

48 Miss Cowie was evidently overly affectionate with the boys, on one occasion, discovered holding Jack in her arms. She was eventually dismissed for such overt displays of affection. Her absence removed another woman from Jack's life and at that pivotal time, the only person who defended him from the boys who already disliked and bullied him.

49 Gastons is the name of the Kirkpatrick's home.

50 Jack, Tolkien, and Dyson had their famous stroll

on Addison's Walk on 19 September 1931, a little over a year after his conversion to theism and only nine days before his Christian conversion.

51 Maureen drove Mrs. Moore and Mrs. Moore's goddaughter, Vera.

52 C.S. Lewis. *They Stand Together: The Letters of C.S. Lewis to Arthur Greeves (1914-1963)*, ed., Walter Hooper (New York: MacMillan Publishing Co., Inc., 1979), 566. © CS Lewis Pte Ltd 1979. Used with permission.

53 Mrs. Moore died as a non-Christian on 12 January 1951 and evidently resented Jack's faith. The selfish mother in *The Great Divorce* may be patterned after her.

54 For a more in-depth look at their relationship, I suggest *Tolkien and C.S. Lewis: The Gift of Friendship* by Colin Duriez.

55 This is particularly true of *That Hideous Strength* and *The Four Loves*.

56 For an in-depth look, consider, *The Oxford Inklings: Lewis, Tolkien and Their Circle* by Colin Duriez.

57 N.W. Clerk is "Nat Whilk," Anglo-Saxon for "I know not whom" and "Clerk" meaning, "a scholar or writer."

58 *The Problem of Pain* (1940) presents Jack's rational, intellectual argument concerning pain. *A Grief Observed* (1961) is Jack's personal, emotional discussion of the same experience.

59 *Spirits in Bondage* (1919) and *Dymer* (1926) were both were published under the pseudonym of Clive

Hamilton.

60 Although not strictly autobiographical, Jack acknowledged in the 1943 revised edition that he had written the book to share his conversion story.

61 Bruce L. Edwards. "C.S. Lewis and the Gospel of Homesickness" in *C.S. Lewis: Life, Works, and Legacy: Volume 4: Scholar, Teacher and Public Intellectual*, ed., Bruce L. Edwards (Westport: Praeger Publishers, 2007), 311.

62 The Ransom Trilogy is comprised of *Out of the Silent Planet* (1938), *Perelandra* (1943) and *That Hideous Strength* (1943).

63 Scientism is the ideology that science is the only valid source of knowledge that alone defines reality and particularly to the exclusion of the supernatural.

64 Jack even coined the phrase "Wellsianity" to define that worldview.

65 The BBC talks made Jack a radio personality whose book sales and popular influence increased as a result. It also increased the resentment exercised by Oxford colleagues and religious leaders.

66 "You can search Time's cover stories 35 weeks forward and backwards and never see another religious figure or spiritual topic featured. Such was the notoriety and impact of Lewis, even 61 years ago." Bruce L. Edwards. "The Devil and Mr. Lewis." http://www.cslewis.com/the-devil-and-mr-lewis/ (Accessed 14 February 2019).

67 Jack is praised and disparaged in both the literary and theological worlds as being too much of one and/

or not enough of the other, but he cannot be ignored in either context.

68 Jack's evangelist intent for *The Chronicles of Narnia* is demonstrated in my book *Ten Things about the Chronicles of Narnia* (forthcoming in this series).

69 Jack was not opposed to science but to scientism as earlier defined.

70 Henry L. Carrigan. "C.S. Lewis: Still Bringing Joy to Readers," *Publisher's Weekly*, 27 March 2013.

https://www.publishersweekly.com/pw/by-topic/industry-news/religion/article/56535-c-s-lewis-still-bringing-readers-joy.html (accessed 14 February 2019).

www.ingramcontent.com/pod-product-compliance
Lightning Source LLC
Chambersburg PA
CBHW052113070526
44584CB00017B/2465